UP
IN THE AIR

CONTENTS

Have you ever looked at the night sky?
Have you ever thought
"I wonder what is up there
high above the earth."
Did you want to learn more?
Well here are the answers
to some questions you might have.

What are stars?

Stars are big balls of burning hot gas.
The burning gas makes heat and light.
You can see stars in the night sky,
but they are a long way away.
The nearest star to Earth is the sun.
But it is 93 million miles
(150 million km) away.
Some stars are blue and white.
They are the hottest stars.
But the sun is only a small yellow star.

Night Sky

Written by Tracey Reeder

Is there air
up there
where the stars
are?

What is a constellation?

Have you ever made patterns out of the stars in the night sky? A constellation is a group of stars that together make a pattern or shape. All the known constellations have names. They are named after animals, or famous people, heroines, or heroes.

Pisces

Mercury

Cetus

Did you know Pegasus was one of the first constellations to be named?

Venus

Look on this page.
What shapes or patterns
can you see?
Can you see an animal
with a triangle for a head?
What other different shapes
can you see?

What is a comet?

A comet is a lump of rock, gas,
ice, and dust that moves
through space.
A comet is made up
of a head and a tail.
The head of a comet has
a nucleus and a coma.
The nucleus is made up
of rocks and ice and the coma
is made up of gases.
As a comet gets nearer
to the sun its tail gets bigger.
The tail gets bigger
because the heat from the sun
changes the ice
in the nucleus into gases.
The heat from the sun
then pushes the gases and dust
from the head into the tail.
As the tail of a comet
gets bigger, the comet moves
faster through space.
A comet's tail always points
away from the sun.

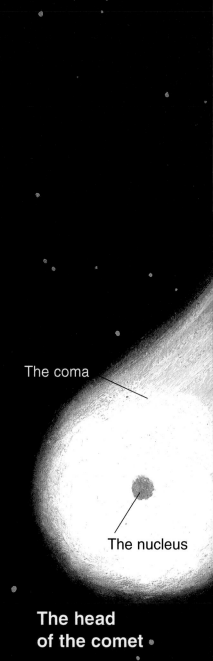

The coma

The nucleus

**The head
of the comet**

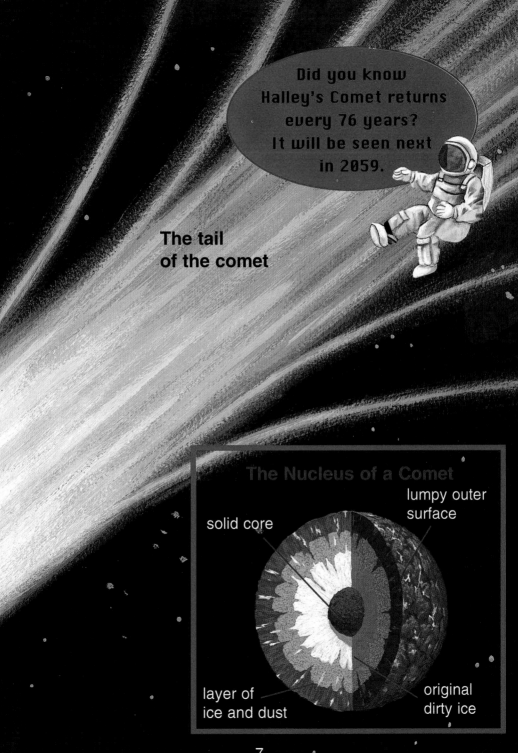

Did you know Halley's Comet returns every 76 years? It will be seen next in 2059.

The tail of the comet

The Nucleus of a Comet

lumpy outer surface

solid core

layer of ice and dust

original dirty ice

A meteorite crater

What is a meteor?

A meteor is a small piece of rock
that moves through space.
Sometimes meteors are called
falling or shooting stars
because they look like they are falling
or shooting through the night sky.
Many meteors are about the size of a pin head.
These little meteors will not reach Earth
as they burn up in Earth's atmosphere.
Very big meteors are called meteorites.
Meteorites can reach Earth.
The biggest meteorite was found in Africa.
It weighed more than 60 tonnes (59 tons).

What is an asteroid?

An asteroid is sometimes called a minor planet
An asteroid is a large piece of rock
that moves around the sun.
There are many asteroids that travel
between the planets Mars and Jupiter.
This part of space is called the asteroid belt
as it is filled with more than 4,000 asteroids.
People think that these asteroids
could have been made
when one of Jupiter's moons blew up.

The next time you look
up into the night sky,
you may be able
to point out
some of these things.

Our Solar

Written by Kerrie Capobianco

Our solar system is made up of the sun
and the planets that move around it.
There are also moons, asteroids, meteors,
and comets in our solar system.

This picture shows our solar system.
It is an oval shape.
Our solar system is just a small part
of a galaxy called the Milky Way.
There are many galaxies in space.
A galaxy is made up
of lots and lots of stars.
The stars are like our sun.

The Sun

The sun is in the middle of our solar system.
It is a star.
It is the biggest thing in our solar system.

Do you think
there are other
solar systems
in the world?
How can you
find out?

THE PLANETS

There are nine planets in our solar system.
Four of these planets are rocky planets.
Four of these planets are gas planets
and one planet is made mostly of ice.

THE ROCKY PLANETS

The four planets closest to the sun
are Mercury, Venus, Earth, and Mars.
They are called the rocky planets,
because the ground on these planets
is like the ground on Earth.

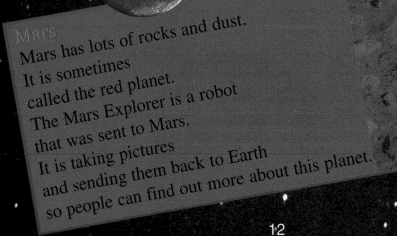

Mars

Mars has lots of rocks and dust.
It is sometimes
called the red planet.
The Mars Explorer is a robot
that was sent to Mars.
It is taking pictures
and sending them back to Earth
so people can find out more about this planet.

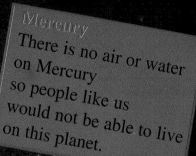

Can you find out why Mars is called the red planet?

Venus
Venus is the brightest planet we can see from Earth. It only takes 224 days for Venus to go around the sun. See if you can see Venus in the night sky. It looks like a bright star.

Mercury
There is no air or water on Mercury so people like us would not be able to live on this planet.

Earth
Earth is the only planet in our solar system that people are able to live on.

THE GAS PLANETS

Four of the planets are called the gas giants.
They are not made of rocks and sand.
They are made of gases.
These planets are the largest planets
in our solar system.

Jupiter
Jupiter is the biggest planet.
It has a big red spot on it.
Sometimes
the red spot moves
around on the planet.
People think that
the red spot is a giant storm.

Neptune

This planet has green and blue clouds around it. It has 8 moons.

Uranus

Did you know that Uranus takes 84 years to go around the sun? It has 17 moons.

Saturn

Saturn
has wide rings
around it.
The rings are made
of ice and dust.
The rings are not joined.
When you look at the rings
from Earth,
they look like they are solid.

Pluto

Pluto is the smallest planet.
It is made up mostly of ice.
Pluto is a very long way
from the sun.
That is why it is so cold.

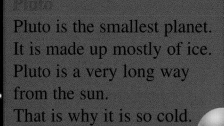

Can you
find out why
the gas planets
are bigger than
the rocky planets?

As far as we know,
Earth is the only planet with life on it.
The other planets in our solar system
do not have the kind of air
that animals and plants need to live.
But there is still a lot to learn
about our solar system.
New things are being found out
all the time.
Maybe one day
we might find life up in the night sky!

DID YOU KNOW?

About 3.5 billion years ago,
the air on Mars
was very different.
People think that there may once
have been life on Mars.

"Mir" is a Russian word. It can mean peace, or world.

18

SPACE

Written by Erin Hanifin

People have been going into space since the 1960s.
When people first went into space,
they could only stay away from Earth
for a few hours.
Later, they could stay away for a few days.
But by the late 1980s, people could go into space
and stay for more than a year.
People lived and went to work on space stations.

Mir is a space station.
Mir is a Russian space station.
People from many different countries
live and work on the Mir Space Station.

LIVING IN SPACE

The Mir Space Station
is made up of many
different areas.
There are areas
for living and working
and for storing things.
It also has an area
where spaceships
come to dock.
This area is called
a docking bay.

Air in space is not the same
as the air on Earth.
Most of the areas in the spaceship
need to have air from Earth
added to them.
Air is needed to keep people alive.
Everything floats around in space.
This is because there is no gravity in space.
Gravity is a force
that keeps people and things on the ground.

Would you like
to live on
a space station?

The living area on the Mir Space Station
is like a home with areas for living
and areas for sleeping.

A galley is used for cooking,
eating, and putting waste.
Cabins are used for sleeping, sitting, and
looking out through windows into space.
There is also a bathroom with toilets
and showers.

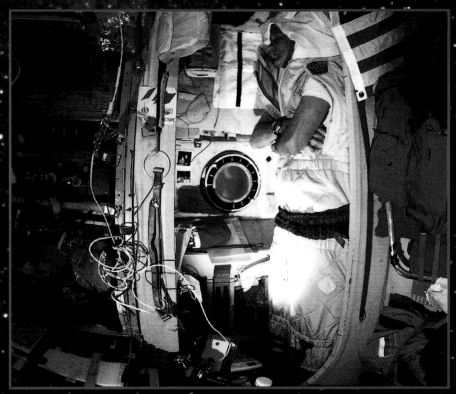

PEOPLE WHO HAVE LIVED IN SPACE

Some of the people who live and work on Mir
have been there for a long time.
Vladimir Titov (Vla di mir Ti tov)
and Musa Manarov (Mu sa Man a rov)
are two Russians.
They were the first people
to live on Mir for more than a year.

A doctor named Valeri Polyakov
(Val e ri Pol yak ov) went to Mir
in September, 1988.
He found that people could live in space
for more than a year and not get sick.
In 1994, Valeri Polyakov went back to Mir
and stayed for 15 months.
This is the longest time
that anyone has stayed in space.

On November 4, 1994, a woman
named Elena Kondakova (Kon da ko va)
went to Mir.
She was the first woman
to live and work on Mir.

Then in 1996, another woman,
named Shannon Lucid, went to Mir.
She was from the United States.
Shannon Lucid stayed on Mir for 188 days.
This was the longest time a woman
or an American had stayed
in space.

Shannon Lucid with two Russian astronauts

Shannon Lucid reading a book

In 1997, Shannon Lucid talked to some children about living and working in space. Here are some of the things the children wrote after her talk.

In the space station, there is an exercise room with a treadmill. They had to wear straps so they wouldn't float off the treadmill. They needed to exercise in space because if they didn't exercise, their legs would not work very well. Their muscles would be wasted.

Harsile Bandhara, age 10

While Shannon was up there, her food went everywhere. When she was eating, they had to use some furry prickly fabric, which held the food together. If they didn't do this, their food would have gone everywhere.

Shahim Siddiqi, age 10

FINDING OUT MORE ABOUT SPACE

There are many ways to find out more about space. You can read more books and use the Internet. You can watch the news on the television, or you can visit a space museum.

Only a few people get the chance to go into space. In the future, will you be one of them?

Ozone

Written by Brian Birchall
Illustrated by Lorenzo Van Der Lingen

What is ozone?

Ozone is a gas.
It is one of the gases
in a layer around Earth.
This layer is called the ozone layer.
You can't see ozone.
You can't touch it.
But people need ozone.
It is very helpful.

How is ozone made?

Ozone is made by the sun.
New ozone is made every day.

Do you know
how ozone is helpful?
Read on to find out.

25

How is the ozone layer helpful?

The ozone layer
is very high above Earth.
The ozone layer is very thin,
but it helps keep people
safe from the sun.
The sun is higher
than the ozone layer.
The sun's rays have to go
through the ozone layer
to get to Earth.
By the time the sun's rays
come through the ozone layer,
they are not as harmful.

How does the sun harm people?

The sun's rays can burn your skin.
That is why you need to wear sunscreen,
or find a place to sit out of the sun.
Under a tree is a good place to sit.

What is happening to the ozone layer?

The ozone layer is changing.
It is getting thinner.
In some places,
the ozone layer is so thin it has holes in it.
This means that the sun's rays are stronger
and more harmful when they get to Earth.

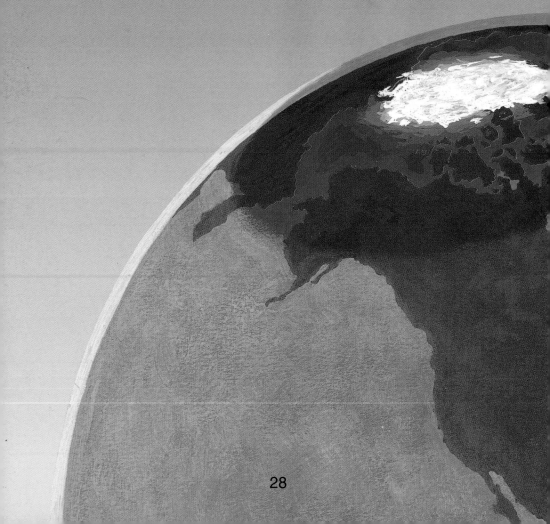

Why is the ozone layer getting thinner?

The ozone layer is getting thinner
because people are using things
that make harmful gases.
Some of the gases get into the air
and move up to the ozone layer.
These harmful gases change the ozone gas.

Do you know
what you might be doing
to harm
the ozone layer?

Where do these harmful gases come from?

The harmful gases
come from lots of things.
Some come from spray cans.
Some come from
the parts of old refrigerators.
And some are made
when you burn your garbage.

What can you do to help the ozone layer?

There are lots of things that you can do to help.
You can change to use sprays that have a pump at the top.
If you send someone a gift, use less packing paper.
Do not burn your garbage.
Put it out to be taken away.
See if you can recycle some of your garbage.
You can tell people to recycle the gases
in their old refrigerators.
All of this will help to save the ozone layer.
All of this will help save you
from the harmful rays of the sun.

WILDCATS
Bobcat

Index